Psalms for the Suffering Church

Psalms for the Suffering Church

JEFFREY A. STONE

RESOURCE *Publications* · Eugene, Oregon

PSALMS FOR THE SUFFERING CHURCH

Resource Publications
An Imprint of Wipf and Stock Publishers
199 W. 8th Ave., Suite 3
Eugene, OR 97401

www.wipfandstock.com

PAPERBACK ISBN: 978-1-6667-4964-9
HARDCOVER ISBN: 978-1-6667-4965-6
EBOOK ISBN: 978-1-6667-4966-3

07/17/22

Larry Kent Stone
1946–2021

Father, Teacher, Mentor, Friend.

Precious in the sight of the LORD
Is the death of his saints.

PSALM 116:15

Contents

1

Lord and Master, Your love for Your people is great.

Greater than the mountain peak, more vast than the savannah.

We pray the prayers our fathers taught us,

We sing the songs of our mother's mother.

Like great birds with winged beauty and lions with clawed strength, we, Your creatures, praise You.

Earth and sky, river and sun, moon and mountain praise You.

Grasshopper and mighty warrior lift up the arms you fashioned for them

All for the sake of your goodness.

As we praise, others laugh. Those who mock Your Name are outside shouting.

Ones who hate You hurl lies like stones with murder in their hearts.

Save us, Abba, from the violence of evil men. Protect us with Your grace.

By Your strong hand and Your mighty arm, save those who love Your words.

All the day, my Father, I will acclaim You and worship You.

Even though I am weak with fear, I will trust You to keep me strong.

Those who hate Your righteousness surround Your house of worship.

They pound on the doors of Your holy temple.

Arrogance fills their hearts and blood is on their hands.

They use bullets and grenades and bombs on Your people.

These are the ones who set violence ablaze to consume the green grass while Your children try to run.

They fear not Your judgment or Your justice.

Save us, Abba, from the violence of evil men. Protect us with Your grace.

By Your strong hand and Your mighty arm, save those who love Your words.

Turn back the evil, Lord, with a gentle wind of grace.

Make the gun to cease and bombs to stop.

Cause the bullets to freeze in the barrels of their rifles;

Make them fall to the earth like harmless rain.

Turn grenades into doves who fly away to rest in the shade.

Save us, Abba, from the violence of evil men. Protect us with Your grace.

By Your strong hand and Your mighty arm, save those who love Your words.

2

The God of Jacob is our rock.
The Jesus who lives is our abode.

We need not the weapons of man.
We take up only and always the sword of God's spirit, His Word.

Place shields in our hands and
Strong breastplates on our chests.

Fit our feet with the Gospel of Life
As Jesus lives in our minds, hearts, and lips.

The God of Jacob is our rock.
The Jesus who lives is our abode.

3

The walls of our church are thin and frail.
Like a widow's blanket.
Like the shoes of our children.

Outside we have no guard.
An old man grey with years,
Welcomes pilgrims who come.

You, O Lord, are the watchman
As we pray, You are our ramparts.
We sing and Your angels protect us.

My brothers may fall at my right
My sisters die at my left
But You are with me as I pray

"Let only the sound of singing remain."

4

Another night passes away in Liuzhoh Prison.

Before the guards come to search the

Cellblock for the sick and deliver the mail,

Dawn-light floods golden in my small room as the

Energy of the sun warms my shrinking body.

Food will be cold today, but it will be enough.

God keeps me in this place; He is the guardian of my soul.

Humanity dies easily here and many do not last the night.

Illness and injury, hunger and hatred threaten to consume.

Jesus Christ is my crime; for speaking His Name above all others,
I am guilty.

King of Kings!

Lord of Lords!

Missionaries of Your kingdom linger in this place

Not knowing when they will feel again the touch of a relative's hand.

O Father, free those who are bound in chains!

Proclaim liberty to those imprisoned for Your sake.

Quietly send us hope to strengthen and encourage us that our trial
is not in vain.

Rally the spirits of Your saints to pray for those who imprison us.

Send us letters and news of home to know that we are not forgotten.

Torture is the weapon of the enemy, but in Your strength we will
endure and be purified.

Unbound we long to be! To rest in the shade of trees. To hug our
children. To praise You.

Valiant are Your saints, O Lord, who endure for the Name of Jesus.

When You grant freedom, save our captors. Turn enemies into brothers.

Xi'an was my home. The city of "Western Peace." May Your shalom now fall on me.

Zealously guard Your people unto eternal life, for You alone are the God who lives.

5

Come and sing with me
All you who love God.
Sing for the love of Christ.
Though for a while you suffer,
He holds your crown safe in
Nail scarred hands.

Come and sing, shout for joy!
All you who love God.

Grazing cattle and flying bird
Gazelle and Lion
Jackal and Hound
Eagle and Ant
Humming river and crashing sea
Proclaim the goodness of Our Father.

Come and sing, shout for joy!
All you who love God.

Your people were oppressed in Egypt.
In Canaan they fought for life.
Israel prayed for relief from evil men.
From all our enemies, You will deliver us.
From prison and fear, O Lord,
Your will rescue Your faithful ones.

Come and sing, shout for joy!
All you who love God.

The ones who hate You believe
They control our lives and deaths.
"Where is your God?"
"Renounce this 'holy one' or die!"
They do not know You.
You sit on Your throne and laugh.

Come and sing, shout for joy!
All you who love God.

You test us like gold;
As the finest gold and purest silver,
Your saints pass through fire.
Our enemies pass through us
As a sickle through the wheat and still
We are not consumed.

Come and sing, shout for joy!
All you who love God.

We are Your grain
Harvested for Holy bread.
Your martyrs and Your Holy Ones
Who overcome by the blood of the Lamb!
Graves and tears no more hold sway!
Only life and love and joy beyond measure.

Come and sing, shout for joy!
All you who love God.

6

Rescue Your beloved!
Come to my aid for I am falling
Into the dust of death.
The sleep of eternity enfolds me in cold arms
While scoffers mock with venomous lips.
You, my God, are my life.
Restore me from the grave and I will praise You.
Take me to Yourself that I may rejoice and sing
At the great wedding feast of the Lamb and His Bride.
Rescue Your Beloved!

7

For the Name of Jesus I will sing.
He found me as a treasure
And hid me in a field.
Selling all He had, He rejoiced to
Buy the field and claim me as His own.

My Lord rejoices over me with singing.
As a cedar of Lebanon, He makes me strong.
Like a rose of Sharon, He makes me beautiful.
How blessed I am that my Jesus won me.

Of Christ, I will sing
And gladly be chained for my beloved.

8

Though crushed,
We conquer.
Though killed,
We rise.
Though nothing,
We are all to Him.
Though weak,
We are strong.
Though dead,
We live.
For we follow in the path of the cross.

9

When you are tempted,
Praise Him.
When the attacks of the foe are strong,
Praise Him.
On the day when enemies attack,
Praise Him.
On the day of your arrest,
Praise Him.
When the mockers mock you,
Praise Him.
When the scoffers throw dust,
Praise Him.
While your captors beat you,
Praise Him.
When the beatings cease,
Praise Him.
In the presence of soldiers,
Praise Him.
In the courts of the magistrates,
Praise Him.
For every cut and scar,
Praise Him.
For every tear and sigh,
Praise Him.
For every orphan and widow,
Praise Him.

For those without refuge,
Praise Him.
Hear the cry of the powerless,
Praise Him.
Hear the prayers of the wounded,
Praise Him.
In grand cathedrals,
Praise Him.
In catacomb churches,
Praise Him.
On the day of execution,
Praise Him.
On the day of freedom,
Praise Him.
When enemies embrace as brothers,
Praise Him.
Praise Jesus, all you peoples,
Who has taught us to bear the cross.

10

Why do the nations plot in vain?
The enemies of Your kingdom fail.
For You, O YHWH our God, are enthroned above all gods.
Your enemies are put to shame.
The plots of the nations come to nothing.

Evil ones conspire to destroy
The martyrs of God with violence.
Christ the Lamb rescues His chosen ones.
His martyrs are clothed with white robes.
Evil ones are put to shame.

Those who hate You yearn for bloodshed.
Your Church suffers their attacks and death,
But Your Holy Spirit gives hope and strength.
Your Church will never be overcome.
The haters will be undone by Your steadfast love.

11

Lord Christ, nothing is hidden from You.
I know my sin and it is a heavy burden on my heart.
Day and night I fill my bed with tears.
I cannot eat or sleep for the shame of my guilt.

Like Paul, I have persecuted You.
I sought the lives of Your Holy Ones
With the name of an idol
On my lips.

My heart was filled with hatred for Your Name.
I despised your righteousness and I
Mocked Your justice. And still, You call me 'Son'.
Bloody hands You make clean.

I weep for my past and the Accuser
Drags me before Your courts.
Shackled and bound, he torments me
With the memories of my sins.

The charges are true!
No escape or denial.
I have sinned against the blood of Your Holy Ones.
It calls out from the ground for justice.

What hope can I have?

None will stand to plead my cause.
I will be food for wolves.
The jackals will tear my flesh.

But You, O Lord, stood up for me.
As my guilt was judged, You stepped forth
With scars and wounds that declared
Your deepest love for me.

I am a sinner redeemed.
The chief sinner saved by Jesus.
A sinner saved by the One he tried to kill.

Dry my tears and calm my soul.
The sin that was in me
Is no more simply because
He loves me.

1 2

Save us, Lord Jesus.
Feed us, Lord Jesus.

Food has become a weapon of war.
The eyes of the hungry are already dead.
The famine kills them before their bodies stop.
Children die in their parent's arms—sleeping, ruined dolls.
The hunger is patient.
A silent, stealthy, brutal hunter who stalks his prey,
With ease and practiced skill.
They are hungry enough to eat the dust.
They are hungry enough to ponder the unthinkable . . .
What living hell is this?
Lives are gnawed away.
They waste and vanish like smoke while the
Soldiers taunt them with the
Deliciously sick smell of their
Cooking fires.

Save us, Lord Jesus.
Feed us, Lord Jesus.

We are starving.

13

The tears of the widow
Drop heavy on the ground.

Water that makes rivers and
Streams in the desert.

Sadness that cries out to You, O YHWH,
Like a brother's blood from the receptive earth.

Your people are brought down
To the depths of Sheol.

In the dust of death,
They dwell in silence.

How long, O Christ,
Until You save us?

How long, O Lord
Until Your justice reigns?

Even though we die,
Under Your altar we will live in safety.

Spread Your wings over us as a
Hen with her chicks.

Your mercy will save us.
In You we have no fear.

Do not tarry, Lord Jesus,
Come quickly with your angels.

The tears of the widow
Drop heavy on the ground.

But You will turn them into
A river of life.

14

Prevent me, O YHWH
From loving the lusty taste
Of vengeance.

Keep my body and mind whole
And my spirit limber
To play in the pneuma of Your mercy.

15

By the rivers of

China . . .
Egypt . . .
Eritrea . . .
India . . .
Iran . . .
Iraq . . .
Kazakhstan . . .
Pakistan . . .
Uzbekistan . . .
Vietnam,

We sat in

Huts . . .
Ditches . . .
Hospitals . . .
Dungeons . . .
Hovels . . .
Jails . . .
Prisons . . .
Basements . . .
Holes . . .
Tombs . . .

And wept as we remembered

Home . . .
Children . . .
Wife . . .
Husband . . .

Friends . . .
Church . . .
Mail . . .
Medicine . . .
Food . . .
Clothes . . .

Our captors toyed with us; they tormented our souls.
"Tell us a story of home.
Sing to us about your god."

Oh, Lord Christ, how can we sing?
How can we speak without tears while
We are in chains for the sake of Your Name?

How cruelly they mock us. How brutally they beat us.
They are without mercy or pity and
They hate Your Law.

Turn their derision back on them. Let their mockery become their
fate!
Blind them with Your justice and then
Forgive them.

Turn their hearts so that   Mercy . . .
                                 Love . . .
                                 Peace . . .
                                 Forgiveness . . .
                                 Healing . . .

Brotherhood . . .
Faith . . .
Compassion . . .
Kindness . . .
Life . . .

Will reign forever.

16

In the morning dawn
I will praise You.
With the rising sun, Your Name
I will acclaim to the nations.

May Your Righteousness
Ring through the mountains.
May the rivers sing Your Justice
And the hills rejoice.

I rise to meet the day
To the glory of the Father
With the salvation of the Son
Under the wings of the Spirit.

As I face the jailer today
Or the inquisitor
Or the executioner
Your Name shall be on my lips.

No one can harm me
Jesus, You hold the keys.
Death is but a sleep
I will rise to life eternal.

In the morning dawn
I will praise Your Name.
At the set of sun
I give glory to You.

17

Sing and make music to YHWH!
With the instruments of men
Make music to Him!

With Guqin and Kissar
Trong and Goema
Let music be made!

With Guitar and Flute
Ruan and Dizi
Praise Him all the day!

Never cease the sound of singing.
Make hymns and melodies sweet
Last through the night!

May the whispered worship
Of Your chained ones
Drown the noise of hell!

Let all Your people sing!
Make music and be glad!
The chant lives forever!

And so will we!
Alleluia!

18

Your love is better than life.
It floods the earth like mighty rivers.
As a flood it covers all
Your creation.

Every moment of the day is
For Your glory.
Every second of time is
For Your honor.

Though evil men surround me
You I will honor.
Though false attackers accuse me
You I will glorify.

O my heart, do not fail,
O my soul, do not weep.
The God of Israel will save you,
The Lamb of God will restore you.

19

Because we are young African girls,
    The West has forgotten us.

Only Your grace has kept us alive,
    And helped us endure a nightmare.

Kindness is not found in our captor's hands
    Who shame us, defile us without mercy.

On a whim, they buy us for pleasure,
    And sell us as child brides to old men.

However we suffer, we will not deny Jesus,
    With our hearts and minds, we remain faithful to Christ.

Alleluias we bring You, most Holy God,
    Our bodies are ravaged; help us to praise and to escape.

Rape and murder are the weapons of the enemy,
    Please protect Your daughters, strong and loving Father.

Attend to our cries for life and
    Break off the manhood of our tormentors. Emasculate them!

May the mountains crush their bodies for the sake of justice,
    So we may begin to heal . . . and forgive.

20

As I consider the works of Your hands, O Lord,
I am amazed at the beautiful variety of creation.
All manner of winged bird and creeping thing
Sings the praise to the wisdom of Your Word.
I consider human beings, and I am awed.
You have made us different in ways that are stunning to behold.
Even those who hate us,
Even the ones who seek our lives are made in Your Image.

They have been blinded by the Enemy, Lord God.
They do not know and they cannot see the truth of Your ways.
Deluded and futile in their thinking they are.

When I think that You have made all people,
Even my enemies,
I have hope.

You do not wish for Your Creation to perish.
You desire Life for all.

Let me, then, follow Your example and
Pray for the ones who will kill me.
Allow me to plead forgiveness for them.
So great is the power of Your redeeming love that
Even my killers are not beyond mercy's grasp.

As I close my eyes to rest in Your arms,
May I open them and see myself surrounded
Not by enemies,
But by brothers.

21

My Lord, My Jesus
My Shepherd, My King

The people who love You are dying.
The suffering of Your children is great.
You have promised to always be near us.
You have promised to never forsake us.

And yet we die by the hand of the enemy.
Their machetes are sharp,
Their malice runs deep as blood.
With violence they attack and we cannot stand.

My Lord, My Jesus
My Shepherd, My King

Even though we die, we will trust in You.
For You have conquered death.
You have banished fear.
You have opened tombs.

Let every nation sing of Your greatness!
Let every people praise Your Name!
Our tears are for but a moment.
Our Joy will be forever.

My Lord, My Jesus
My Shepherd, My King

Our blood has been spilt on beaches.
In prisons we have suffered.
In our churches we have been shot.
And yet the Enemy cannot kill us!

Let our blood cry out in Joy.
Let our prison cells be filled with singing.
May our churches explode with praise.
For our foes have only brought us to Life.

My Lord, My Jesus
My Shepherd, My King

Crown Your martyrs with righteousness,
As You once were crowned with thorns.
Forgive those who take our lives,
Even as You forgave.

Show grace and mercy.
For only through love will
The circle of violence be broken.
And Your Shalom, at last, cover the Earth.

My Lord, My Jesus
My Shepherd, My King

22

Oh God, my God,
I am angry with You!
My father was faithful to You.
My mother sang Your songs to me in my cradle.
They whispered Your Name in
My ear all the day.

When I laid down,
And when I arose.
As I came and as I went.
As we walked and sat.
At the table my parents spoke of
Your grace and mercy.

They taught their children
To love You and hear Your Word with gladness.
Your Law and Your Gospel were always
On their minds, lips, and hearts.
They loved You more than life
And they loved me with joy.

And now evil men have attacked them.
With guns and knives they
Shoot and slash until the air is
Full of smoke and fear and the smell of blood.

My mother is gone; My father is dying
I can only pray and cry and close his eyes.

I am angry at You Lord!
You knew these men would come!
How hard would it be for You
To stop them from doing violence?
If nothing is beyond Your power,
Then why this great sadness, loss, and senseless death?

My mother prayed every day.
My father was always faithful.
They looked to you for protection.
And now we gather at this cemetery.
My father is dead.
My mother is taken from me.

Why did You not save them?
Were You unwilling?
Were You unable to rescue?
My God, I am weary from crying!
I am worn to nothing by sorrow!
My faith in You is but a thread.

But from the slender threads of grief, You weave
A garment of life and beauty.
My faith right now is small, Lord Jesus,
But I still believe that You are the Christ.

I tie myself to Your promises and I
Pray You, please forgive my anger.

Death came in an instant
But life with You is forever.
Lord God, I am hurting and angry.
But Lord, to whom else shall I go?
Only You have the Words
Of eternal life.

23

Create in me a clean heart, O God

> Yes, Lord, for my heart is filled with hurt.
>
> Wicked men have attacked my church and
>
> Those who hate You are violent against Your people.
>
> Ease my pain with the comfort of Your grace.
>
> Forgive my anger and my thirst for vengeance.
>
> A clean heart in me create.

And renew a right spirit within me

> Yes, Lord, for my spirit is broken by bloodshed.
>
> Children have died and parents suffer loss.
>
> Your beautiful ones are captured for torture and rape.
>
> The orphans are many.
>
> It destroys the spirit to see such evil.
>
> Yes, Lord, renew my soul!
>
> A spirit of love, joy, mercy, and forgiveness give me.
>
> That I may embrace the wicked in mercy.
>
> A new spirit in me create.

Cast me not away from Your Presence

> Yes, Lord, keep me close to You.
>
> The roaring lion moves quickly against me.
>
> Without You, I will fall prey to temptation and
>
> Hope will leave me.
>
> You have promised to never forsake Your children.

I need You now.

Cast not Your poor servant away.

Take not Your Holy Spirit from me

    Yes, Lord, Your Spirit sustains me.

    Your Spirit filed Adam with life.

    Your breath floods over dry bones and

    The dead stand like a might army.

    In deserts and jungles, Your people perish.

    In prisons and forgotten places, Your people languish.

    With Your Holy Spirit, Lord, bring them to life.

    With Your Holy Spirit, breathe on me.

Restore to me the joy of Your salvation

    Yes, Lord, for joy has been driven from my heart.

    Every day I endure pain and witness destruction.

    Your precious ones are loaded into boats of

    Molded wood and brittle steel to flee the

    War zones with nothing but their lives.

    Remind me again of Your salvation

    That I may rejoice in the Risen One,

    Who was the Lamb once slain.

    In Him, Lord, restore my joy.

And uphold me with Your free spirit.

    Yes, Lord, for my spirit lingers in this world.

    With every lost life,

    With every gun, bomb, bullet, and knife,

    My spirit fades away.

But You, O YHWH are my rock!
You, O Christ, are the anchor for my soul!
Keep me close to You and
I will praise Your mercy all the day.
Yes, Lord, with Your free spirit, uphold me.

24

Dearest Jesus
You have sent us forth to sing Your Name and
To tell of Your righteous deeds of salvation.
But we are sheep amidst the wolves.
For Your sake, we stand before the
Kings, governors, dictators, warlords,
And petty thugs of this world,
Only for the glory of Your Name.
That our lips may testify to You,
Strengthen us.
That our witness may be clear,
Encourage us.
In our chains, help us to stand.
In our death, help us to live,
Dearest Jesus.

25

"Take up your cross and follow me"

What shall we say to this Your word, O Lord?
You bid us to come and suffer like You.
How greatly is Your command fulfilled in us!
As we follow You, Lord, Teacher, Master, Savior
We endure
Beatings, torture, hunger, cold,
Loneliness, isolation, and thirst,
For the sake of Your Name.

It is not our strength that keeps us walking.
You are with us all the day and we stand under Your cross.
We patiently testify, we humbly submit to You.
We are glad to follow in Your footsteps,
O Living Christ, for they lead us from
The bonds of the earth to our home
That You have prepared for those
Who follow You.

26

Sing to the Lord, all you saints!

Sing to the Father who made you!
Sing to the Son who saves you!
Sing to the Spirit who fills you!

With mighty deeds of righteousness
You save.
With Your strong right hand of justice
You conquer.
With cross and thorn and utmost suffering
You redeem.

Sing to the Lord, all you saints!

Though you suffer for a while,
God will not fail you.
Even through the dark valley of death,
My Jesus will not abandon you.

The enemies of God stalk us,
But You rescue.
The lovers of violence prey on us,
But You shield us.

Sing to the Lord, all you saints!

If we are weeping,
You dry our tears.
If we are hopeless,
You restore us.

When hateful ones kill us,
Help us to forgive.
When wicked ones harm and murder us,
Help us to embrace.

Sing to the Lord, all you saints!

27

When You, mighty Father, touch
The mountain peaks,
They crumble.

The earthquake of Your presence
Breaks the hills in pieces
Upon us.

The heights of Makalu cover us.
The top of Manaslu,
Swallows us

Have mercy on Your servants.
For the sake of Your mercy,
Save us.

Send us aid from our brothers
And sisters of the churches to
Feed us.

Send those skilled in rescue
With equipment and courage to
Find us.

Send preachers to preach and
Prayers to pray that You will
Heal us.

Upon the wicked and the good,
Upon the blessed and the cursed,
The mountains fell.

We repent of our sins.
We call upon Your mercy to
Forgive us.

Remove from our hearts the rubble of
Arrogance and the ruins of
Our pride.

Put Makalu back in its place.
Set Manalu back on its base and
Restore us.

Lord Jesus, hear our prayer.
From the brash and scree,
Free us.

Weeping in the debris remains for a time,
But with Your forgiveness You wipe away
Every tear.

28

My God and Lord,
You level the mountains and make the
Rough places smooth.
At Your touch the earth flourishes.
With Your breath, You slay the wicked.
You sweep them away like chaff
In the hot east wind.

My Lord, Your people suffer
Greatly from those who love violence.
Black are their hearts and evil are their deeds.
They do not call upon You to bless.
They spit Your Name as a curse on the ground.

With their boots they break the backs of
Our children.
Their arms are full of savagery.
Their hands are filled with deadly weapons.
Children and the elderly are not safe, Lord.
They die and are thrown into prisons.

Our beautiful ones are shamed.
With lust enemies defile their bodies.
Our hearts are broken with sadness,
And hot tears flow as mighty waters
Down scared faces.

Our hope feels so small, Lord.
Our enemies are so strong
They ride us down into Sheol

But our small hope is in Your greatness.
In You, Lord Jesus, we place our lives,
Our children and our children's children!
Even though death take us,
And our bodies be wounded and striped,
You will not let us fall forever.

Come quickly Lord, that we may praise You.
That we may rise at Your command.
That we may live again.
Come quickly, Lord Jesus.

29

Alabaster tomb
Dirges sung for Pharaoh's son
Nearby, birth cry, "Free!"

Beach with twenty-one
Waves flow out red with witness
Witness Life flow in

Churches shot with guns
Death silenced many voices
Songs of Life still sung

Drunk on martyr's blood
Babylon rises to feast
Quickly save us Lord

Effortless, grace flows
On the heads of chosen ones
Like water and blood

Foundation is laid
Upon the chief cornerstone
Set in Calvary

Garden prayer at night
Prayed by the suffering flock
Answer is the same

Holy skin stripes
Shared by those who follow Him
Wounds mark path to Life

Immortal Infant
Born lowly in House of Bread
Infant saints You feed

Jubilee day comes
For martyrs dressed in white robes
Great Sabbath rest won

Knelt before the sword
Evil tries to extinguish
New Life with one swing

Linger here with us
Behind our prison walls praying
That You will open

Morning light brings Joy
Drive the dark of fear away
You are strong to save

Nails hold fast to wood
Love beyond the deep shadow
Open arms of Christ

Observe Calvary
Rocky skull of suffering
By death He triumphant

Poverty's howling
Thundering through the wire gates
From throats of babies

Quiet hush descends
Young martyrs chosen for death
With tears, we forgive

Remember to weep
Tears for violence victims
Lord Jesus come soon

Sacrificial Son
Lay bound to wood on altar
Soon, nails will bind Him

Terror strikes us down
Deadly traps spring upon us
Safely lead us home

Up through clouds of smoke
Rise the prayers of Your wounded
Incense for altar

Victorious Christ
Power over death proclaim
For Your stricken flock

While You gather us
Under Your merciful wings
With scars, we praise You

Xeric winds blow hot
On martyr's bones low in dust
Spirit bring to Life

Young saints enter Life
Surrounded by witness cloud
Chains broken, run free

Zion our home above
Mansion homes amid the clouds
Shalom covers all

30

Praises be to God the Father!
> In love He created us.
> In love He sustains us.

Praises be to God the Son!
> In love He saved us.
> In love He conquered death.

Praises be to God the Spirit!
> In love He guides us.
> In love together He binds us.

Praised be to God the Trinity!
> In love He saves us though we die.
> In love we die and forever we live.

31

It lurks around corners,
It slinks in the shadows.

Threatening to devour us,
To put out our light,
And extinguish our hope.

It hopes to frighten with death.
It longs to shock with the grave.

Evil has no power enslave us.
Christ the Lamb has triumphed.
He holds the Keys forever.

32

Blessed is the man who waits for You.
Blessed is the woman who hopes in Christ.
They are like the mighty mountains that cannot be moved.
Their roots go deep into the heart of the earth, strong and stable.
The woman possessing Christ has everything.
The man with God holds all in his hands.

The wicked ones have nothing.
Hatred gives no wisdom.
Violence has no understanding.
They are unstable like water—roiling and railing like a stormy sea.

Let their waves, billows, and breakers roll—they cannot last.
Let their tide rise quickly and the surge pour over the walls—they
will come to nothing.
All their evil ambitions will fail.

For there shall come a day when the Almighty will arise.
The Captain of my Soul will appear to safely pilot me home.
With the voice of rushing waters, with the sound of mighty rivers
He will raise His hand in blessing and say,
"Peace. Be still."

33

You who suffer, weep no more.
You who reel under the cross, rejoice.
The day of salvation is at hand and
The hour of rescue is near.

The love of the Savior has come to you
The care of the Shaddai has arrived.

On the day of His birth, the angels sang.
At His first breath, creation clapped its hands.
The strong seas stormed their approval and
The ocean depths swirled with delight.

The love of the Savior has come to you
The care of the Shaddai has arrived.

On the darkest of Fridays, the heavens were silent.
At the blackest of hours, the Father wept.
The foundations of the world shook with sorrow and
The stone of the tomb was rolled shut.

My Lord, You have suffered in Your body.
My God, You have bled and died.
You felt the slaps of shame and
You endured the bashings of hate.

Because You have suffered, we are saved,
For Your love covers us like water.
Because You have risen from the grave,
Your holy ones rejoice with great joy.

The love of the Savior has come to you
The care of the Shaddai has arrived.

When we suffer in prisons, You are with us.
When we are beaten for Your sake, we share in Your scars.
When we are killed under Your cross,
You raise us to life eternal.

O, my soul, do not despair.
O, my heart, be not dismayed.
Your victory is risen from the dead and
Your life is restored by the Christ.

34

My God, evil men have surrounded me.

Wicked ones have encircled my home and my church.

With guns and bombs and knives,

They threaten the lives of Your saints.

Those who mock Your justice are swift to shed blood.

The ones who despise Your righteousness are quick to be violent.

O Lord, save Your people.

O Christ, rescue Your saints.

O Lord, save the ones who love You.

With Justice Lord, strike the teeth of mockers.

With Your recompense, break the arm of the oppressor and the tyrant.

May Your children sing.

May Your saints sing songs of victory in the land.

Throw horse and rider into the sea once more!

Cast the serpent into the fiery lake!

Let them harm Your people no more.

Let them kill Your people no longer.

Judge with your Justice, O Divine Warrior-Prince

That we may rest in Your Shalom.

35

Your people do not suffer in this place.
By the world's standards we are rich and over-fed.
Schools, hospitals, food and clothing abound everywhere.
We have a rich abundance of material things in our
Safe, suburban church.
And for the good things, the wealth, the peace, the plenty we give
thanks.
We are truly grateful.

And yet . . .

Something stirs.
We feel the subtle, probing attacks of the Enemy.
Against us, the Evil One paces and roars around us
Looking, seeking, searching, sneaking for a way in Your house.
Like a thief, like a robber, like a murderer of souls.

He knows our weaknesses—sowing the seeds of doubt and mistrust.
We make idols of money, our homes, our kids, and our selves.
Daily, satan drags his hand-crafted temptations before us.
Little do we know that his delightful traps
Are filled with sharpened blades.
We clamp down and our mouths are
Raked with barbed hooks.

What dangers surround us, Lord!
That our love may grow cold; That our zeal will wither.
That the passion for the Gospel will die.

Lord Jesus, we pray a most dangerous prayer!
Quicken our love; kindle our zeal; enliven our passion.
Let Your House and Your gifts be our deepest desire.
Make us long for Your Word and Sacraments.
Remove from us the idols, the sins and the stumbling blocks.
Take away our self-laid snares and the bitterness of grudges.

On to our hearts, pour the fire of Your Law!
On to our heads, pour the wine of Your Gospel!
Though we have not yet shed our blood,
By what we suffer, teach us to have faith,
So when the Day of testing comes we may stand faithful
And enter the courts of our King with praise and
Go into His gates with singing.

36

O God, my God,
In the day of my trouble,
I called to You.

I prayed for Your provision
In the hour of my affliction,
My Lord and my God that You would save me.

You heard my cry,
And from your abundance,
You lavish gifts on Your servant.

You save the ones who love You
With the bounty of your grace.
You have listened to my prayer.

With great joy I will adore You.
Your awesome deeds I will proclaim.

37

Shepherd Your people Lord
For I cannot.
The task is too great and
My strength is too small.

Your sheep
Flock to me all day long.
So hungry to be fed,
They bite and nip and paw at my soul.

Among the sheep, my Lord, are
False brothers clothed in deceit.
They speak like a cooing dove and
They bite with lion's teeth.

Rescue me God,
For my strength is failing!
Come near to me Jesus,
For no one understands.

They tell me, "Be strong!"
They pat my back and say, "Take heart!"
My heart is poured out like wax.
My faith is bruised reed.

Inside I carry the secrets of my heart and
The burden of sin weighs me down.
The guilt in my mind burns day and night and
My inner thoughts are lead in my soul.

The more I give,
The more they take.
They more they take,
The more I give.

I am burdened by constant caring.
Their griefs have become my own.
I am full of all their troubles,
With no room left for my own.

I have not the strength anymore.
From the attacks of enemies,
From the arrows of the evil one,
I cannot defend myself.

While I am weak the false ones
Hiss and bite at me.
They see the holes in my armor
And strike me down.

O great Shepherd, you have mercy
On your wandering sheep.
Do you yet have mercy and care
Even for me?

Come and save your hurting servant!
Arise and heal your broken one!

38

In the darkness of night,
     I dream of your eternal day.

I am lonely Lord Jesus,
     I long for Your embrace

To sit at Your table, surrounded by many brothers,
     I wait for such a day of joy.

39

In the days of my poverty,
You give me treasure of infinite worth.

As hunger gnaws my body,
You have a banquet prepared for me.

When my eyes grow dark,
You are the Light of the world.

My clothes are threads.
You give me the finest of robes.

The enemies surround me.
You are my mighty fortress.

My friends and family abandon me.
You call me beloved.

My father is killed.
You call me son.

My mother was taken.
You gather me like a hen.

In every moment of loss,
You are my great gain.

In the hour of my death,
You are my life unending.

40

Let my words cease now
That Your Spirit may intercede for us
In the Holy Silence of
Your grace.

Amen.